Warkworth Castle

NORTHUMBERLAND

HENRY SUMMERSON MA, PhD, FSA, FRHS

Warkworth Castle is one of the most impressive examples in Britain of an aristocratic fortified residence. It is a large, complex and ancient structure. Every century from the twelfth to the twentieth has left its mark upon it. Its development meant that it came to comprise, in effect, two castles, one laid out round the outer bailey, and the other in the keep. The latter reproduces many of the components of the former. For all these reasons Warkworth Castle is difficult both to explain and to understand.

This handbook is divided into seven chapters, starting with a brief history of the medieval castle, from its beginnings to the reign of Henry VIII. Then comes a chapter explaining what purposes a castle like Warkworth was intended to serve, and how it fitted into the life of society round it, during the Middle Ages.

Next is a descriptive tour of the buildings in the outer bailey, and as part of this many of the points raised in the first two chapters are taken further, as an aid to the appreciation of the various structures as you examine them. After that is the tour of the keep, but with a difference – the keep and life in it are described as if you were visiting it in 1532.

Following an account of the hermitage, half a mile down the River Coquet, and a brief chapter on the village, the guide concludes with a short history of the castle between the sixteenth century and the present day.

ENGLISH HERITAGE • LONDON

Contents

Unless otherwise stated illustrations are copyright English Heritage and the photographs were taken by the English Heritage Photographic Section

Published by English Heritage
23 Savile Row, London W1S 2ET
© Copyright English Heritage 1995
First published 1995, reprinted 1996, 2001, 2003
Printed in England by St Ives Westerham Press
C80 09/03 02721
ISBN 1 85074 498 X

Chronological Table

The River Coquet makes a peninsula of Warkworth. The castle is on high ground on the left and the church can be seen on the far side of the village. The late fourteenth-century fortified bridge is on the right

The lords of Warkworth are shown in **bold** type and changes to the castle in *italic*

c1150 First castle built by **Henry, Earl of Northumberland** (d1152); *curtain walls, great hall*
1154 Accession of Henry II
1158 Warkworth given to **Roger fitz Richard**
1170 Murder of Becket
1173 Anglo-Scottish hostilities, castle captured
1178 Robert fitz Roger
1199 Accession of King John
1214 John fitz Robert. *Gatehouse, Carrickfergus Tower, other domestic buildings*
1215 Magna Carta
1249 Robert fitz Robert. *Great hall rebuilt*
1264-67 Barons' War
1272 Accession of Edward I
1292 Edward I visits Warkworth
1296 Start of Anglo-Scottish Wars
1310 John fitz Robert

1311 Agreement for future transfer of Warkworth to the Crown
1314 Battle of Bannockburn. *Grey Mare's Tail Tower*
1327 Warkworth twice attacked by Scots
1332 Warkworth granted to **Henry Percy II**
1346 Battle of Neville's Cross
1348-49 Black Death
1352 Henry Percy III
1368 Henry Percy IV – created Earl of Northumberland 1377
1381 Peasants' Revolt
1388 Hotspur captured at Battle of Otterburn. *Keep*
1399 Henry IV usurped the throne
1403 Revolt of Percys. Hotspur killed at Shrewsbury
1405 John Duke of Bedford given Warkworth after it was besieged and captured by Henry IV
1408 Death of first earl
1415 Battle of Agincourt
1416 Henry Percy, second earl. *Collegiate church begun*
1455 Henry Percy, third earl. Start of War of the Roses. Second earl killed
1461 Third earl killed at Battle of Towton
1464 John Nevill, Earl of Northumberland. *Montague Tower*
1471 Henry Percy, fourth earl. *Heightening of Lion Tower*
1485 Battle of Bosworth
1489 Henry Percy, fifth earl
1513 Battle of Flodden
1527 Henry Percy, sixth earl
1532 The earl spent Christmas at Warkworth
1536 Pilgrimage of Grace
1537 Death of sixth earl. Percy lands pass to the crown
1557 Thomas Percy, seventh earl
1558 Accession of Elizabeth I
1569 Rising of the Northern Earls
1569-70 Warkworth ruined by Sir Thomas Forster
1574 Henry Percy, eighth earl
1585 Henry Percy, ninth earl
1588 Defeat of Spanish Armada
1603 Death of Queen Elizabeth. Union of Crowns of England and Scotland
1605 Gunpowder Plot
1616 Death of Shakespeare
1617 James I visited Warkworth
1632 Algernon Percy, tenth earl
1642-45 First Civil War
1649 Execution of Charles I
1660 Restoration of Charles II
1668 Jocelyn Percy, eleventh earl
1672 Building materials from Warkworth given to John Clarke

Warkworth Castle in the Middle Ages

The First Earl of Northumberland's Oath from "Histoire du Roy d'Angleterre, Richard II"

Warkworth is an old place, first recorded in the early eighth century. But there was no castle here until the mid-twelfth century. The earliest fortress appears to have been the work of Earl Henry of Northumberland, the son of David I, King of Scots (1124–53), at a time when the North of England was part of his father's realm. Probably a simple structure at first, of the type known as motte and bailey, this castle would have consisted of an earth mound (the motte) where the keep now stands and a palisaded enclosure (the bailey), itself protected by a deep ditch, in front of it. On its eastern side the bailey extended some way outside the line of the later curtain wall. Such a castle was well placed to defend the southern approaches to the crossing of the River Coquet, at a point where it makes a great loop around the village (see page 3).

A fortified bridge would later give protection to the village against attacks from the north. In 1157, however, Henry II (1154–89) recovered Northumberland from the Scots, and in the following year gave Warkworth, with its castle, to Roger FitzRichard, whose descendants held it until the early fourteenth century. Roger seems to have begun to build a stone castle. It was too weak to resist a Scottish invasion in 1173, when it was captured without difficulty. But work continued under Roger's son, Robert FitzRoger, an important agent of King John (1199–1216), who became rich by royal service and spent some of his gains on the gatehouse and other structures. By the middle of the thirteenth century the chronicler Matthew Paris could describe Warkworth as a noble castle.

Building work went on during the thirteenth century, and by 1292 Warkworth was grand enough to be able to accommodate a royal visit, when Edward I (1272–1307) spent a night here. But the descendants of Robert FitzRoger (who were also known as Claverings, from an estate in Essex) were increasingly burdened by debt, maybe incurred when spending money on architecture, and the beginning of the Anglo-Scottish wars in 1296 added to their difficulties, not least because the castle then had to be manned by troops. In 1319 it was held by a garrison of twenty-four soldiers, with all the usual staff, such as cooks, servants and armourers. Half of those men were being paid by the King, who in 1311 had made a deal with the Claverings, giving them estates in southern England in exchange for Warkworth and their other properties in Northumberland.

The deal became fully effective only when the last Clavering died in 1332, but the King was increasingly in control of

Warkworth well before then.

In 1327 the castle was twice besieged by the Scots. Perhaps Edward III (1327–77) realised that Warkworth was too far from Westminster for him to be able to defend it properly, for in 1332 he granted it to Henry de Percy II, lord of Alnwick, so bringing the castle into the hands of the family with which it would thereafter be inseparably associated.

Originally a great Yorkshire family, though with important estates further south, the Percys came to dominate Northumberland so completely that it could be said that its people "knew no prince but a Percy." Although they already had a major castle at Alnwick when they were given Warkworth, the Percys resided regularly at both, often coming to Warkworth for the winter. Henry de Percy II and Henry de Percy III both died there, in 1352 and 1368 respectively, and they were responsible for important additions to the fabric, notably the construction of the Grey Mare's Tail Tower on the east side, and alterations to the Carrickfergus Tower, the solar and the chapel in the southwest corner. But the most striking addition was made late in the fourteenth century, when Henry de Percy IV, first Earl of Northumberland, had the magnificent keep built, quite probably by the great Durham master mason John Lewyn.

Greatly enriched by his office of Warden of the March, and by his second marriage, to Maud de Lucy, which brought him the lordship of Cockermouth in Cumberland, the first earl had ambitions extending beyond architecture. These ruined him, and very nearly ruined the Percys too. Having helped to depose Richard II (1377–99), he turned against Henry IV (1399–1413) as well. But in the rebellion which broke out in 1403, the earl's son, Henry Hotspur, was killed at

Shrewsbury, and Warkworth was later battered into surrender by seven volleys of the King's cannon, something it was not equipped to resist. The earl's estates were declared forfeit (he himself was killed in battle in 1408), and Warkworth passed back into the King's hands.

Henry IV ruled the North through a son, John, Duke of Bedford, who often resided at Warkworth. But it was hard to govern the region without the family which, in a local chronicler's words, "have the hertes of the people by North, and ever have had," and Henry V (1413–22) brought the Percys back, starting with Hotspur's son, yet another Henry. It was the second earl who planned the collegiate church across the outer bailey, no doubt intending it to be the family mausoleum. It was never finished because both he and his son, the third earl, loyal to the Lancastrian dynasty which had reinstated them, were killed in the Wars of the Roses and buried elsewhere.

Again the estates were forfeited, and again an outsider was installed at Warkworth, this time John Neville (the brother of Warwick the Kingmaker, who made the castle his base for campaigns against Lancastrians in the early 1460s), who was briefly Earl of Northumberland and later Marquess Montague, and who built or rebuilt the Montague Tower at the southeast corner of the castle. Neville changed his title because Edward IV (1461–83), like Henry V, found that he could not rule effectively in the Borders without Percy assistance. And so in 1470 a fourth Percy earl was installed at Warkworth, where he completed the Montague Tower, and where he came to hunt in the park on the west side of the castle, across the river.

The next earl, the fifth, preferred to live in Yorkshire, though he occasionally spent money on repairs at Warkworth, as when part of the wall between the western postern and the keep fell down in 1520. But the sixth earl – Henry, like all his predecessors – made frequent and lengthy visits. He rebuilt the curtain wall between the Montague Tower and the gatehouse, and carried out numerous minor repairs. But his health was always poor, he could not get on with his wife and his brothers, and when he died in 1537 he left all his possessions to Henry VIII (1509–47). Royal officers sometimes resided at Warkworth and kept the castle in repair, but things were never the same again.

The Castle and its Place in Society

Mounted hunter with two dogs pursuing a stag. From Queen Mary's Psalter (early fourteenth century). Landowners' sons often learnt to hunt in their early teens

Warkworth Castle was a fortified residence, built to withstand a siege – as now and then it had to. But that was not all it was. A great castle was also a centre of its lord's local authority, and as such a visible expression of his greatness, and it was designed to serve that purpose also. Contrary to what some people might think, the Percys were not just wild men of the North, with a taste for pillage and battle. Even Hotspur was noted for his courtesy. The earls and their sons were indeed leaders in war. But as the greatest landowners in Northumberland, with lordships based upon Alnwick, Langley, Prudhoe and Beanley as well as Warkworth, and with huge estates in Cumberland and Yorkshire as well as further south, they were leaders in peacetime too. Local society revolved round them and their castles, and Warkworth was a regional court quite as much as it was a military stronghold.

Local landowners might send their sons to be brought up in the earl's household, where they served as pages and learnt polite behaviour (hence "the chamber the boyes lay in" recorded in the keep in about 1560). According to the early fifteenth-century chronicler John Hardyng, himself a servant of the Percys, such an upbringing meant first of all, from the age of four, learning how to read and write, and then acquiring social graces: "To daunse and synge and speke of gentlenese." At fourteen these youths would learn to hunt; only when they were sixteen were they trained for war.

The rooms in the Percys' Yorkshire residences were painted with mottos, proclaiming the importance of prudence and moderation, the need to show kindness to strangers, the superiority of patience to vengeance, and cautioning against excessive reliance on such vanities as rich apparel, great estates and high birth. Above all, they advised, "Drede God and fere thy kynge."

This was an intensely hierarchical society, in which everybody had a fixed place, even the Percys (who in the Middle Ages suffered more often for loyalty than for treason to the Crown – the second, third and fourth earls all died by violence in their Kings' service). As the Earls of Northumberland gave reverence to those above them, so they expected the same from those below. There was nothing shameful about serving the earl or wearing his livery; on the contrary, one gained in standing by serving a great man, by doing so one reflected a little of his glory. But that glory could quite easily become tarnished by neglect, and if a noble was to maintain his authority he had to live in a manner which proclaimed his status. The state and ceremony with which medieval aristocrats conducted their lives seem almost incredible nowadays when one tends to equate pomp with pomposity.

For instance, when the earl got up in the morning, in a bedchamber in which the grooms should have already made up a fire, he would be waited on by one of his gentlemen ushers, who had received the earl's clothes for the day, "fair folded in a sheet," from one of the yeomen of the wardrobe. Another groom would hold the clothes, and the usher would then help the earl to dress. The same attendance, the same formality of procedure, followed when the earl went to chapel, when he ate his breakfast, dinner and supper, and when he went to bed. Nor were things very different for the earl's men; they, too, were expected to lead lives marked by decorum and mutual civility (it was a male-dominated world, and practically all the inmates of a castle such as Warkworth would have been men, the only exceptions being the women who staffed the laundry and a very few attendants upon the countess when she was in residence).

Appearances were important in such a world. In spite of mottos like those quoted above, on important occasions the nobility went all out to impress. They could put out a splendid array of plate, or, in keeping with the medieval taste for bright colours, wear striking clothes. Hotspur must have looked magnificent when he wore "a scarlet mantle, its collar embroidered with pearls, furred with fine ermine, twelve yards broad," over a surcoat blazoned with the arms of the Lucys and the Percys, "the pikes made of great pearls and the lions embroidered in blue silk." Things were not thus all the time, but lords could still make an effect when they took the road, in a great cavalcade of outriders, baggage men and retainers, or when they gave hospitality to strangers.

A lord's hall, where he sat with his followers and dependants, was a powerful symbol of his authority. But one should not think of it as a scene of drunken revelry. Only at great feasts, when the plate was brought out and there might be entertainers, such as the minstrel and tumbler recorded at Warkworth in 1477, was the diet likely to be anything more exciting than bread, ale, fish and mutton. And to make sure that the company behaved itself, ushers would have patrolled the hall, calling out "speak soft, my masters," if the celebrations looked like becoming too noisy. A restrained magnificence was the effect usually aimed at, in lifestyle and buildings alike.

No representation surviving from the Middle Ages gives a more vivid impression of an aristocratic feast than the illumination which the Limbourg brothers painted for "Les Très Riches Heures du Jean Duc de Berry" early in the fifteenth century. The first Earl of Northumberland would probably not have dined in state quite as grand as this, but he would have come as close to it as his means permitted. In an age when peasants are shown in art huddled beside their tiny hearths, the duke has a fire so huge that he needs a screen to protect him from its blaze, and is sheltered from draughts by a fur hat and a magnificent robe which spills out on to the floor on the far side of the table. He eats in a room the floor of which is covered not with rushes but with finely woven straw mats, while the wall behind him is hung with tapestries showing scenes of battle – perhaps a reminder that the nobility justified their privileges by reference to their leadership in war. When many go hungry, the duke allows his little dogs to run over the tablecloth and nibble the food, while he sits in the middle of a table which is raised above the rest of the room by the height of a low dais, his status further emphasised by the canopy over his head. There is nobody sitting next to him, the only other person seated, a bishop, has two empty places between the duke and himself, and his humble gesture shows that he is well aware how great is the social gap which separates him from his host, and how fortunate he is to be eating at the same table.

Behind the duke stands his steward, holding his staff of office. It is the steward's job to keep order in the hall and to oversee the organisation of the feast, and it is he, not the duke, who calls to the men entering the room to draw near. Like everybody else in this scene these newcomers proclaim their rank by their clothes. They are clearly nobles, and will probably be seated to the duke's left, perhaps next to the young man in a fur hat who talks to the duke over the latter's left shoulder. The attendants, too, are men of high rank – the greater the noble, the more important are the men who wait upon him, especially on special occasions like this. On the side of the table opposite to the duke two of these aristocratic waiters, each with a beautiful white towel over his shoulder, attend to the food, some of which has been served on gold plates.

The duke has yet to drink anything, and has no goblet in front of him, but no doubt he will quench his thirst when the young man in a deep blue gown has finished tasting the wine to make sure it is not poisoned. Over this man's right shoulder can be seen a splendid display of gold plate. Only a man of exceptional wealth could afford such a show, to say nothing of the great gold salt cellar which is set directly in front of the duke. All who sat on the other side of this were in every sense "below the salt." One can picture the tables at which lesser men ate, stretching down the hall away from that at which the duke sits. Wearing the duke's livery – his badges of bear and swan can be seen on the canopy above him – and eating his bread, it seems certain that they will feel proud to serve a man of his greatness.

Descriptive Tour of the First Castle

The gatehouse and the bridge (originally a drawbridge) over the dry moat

The Gatehouse

You can get some idea of the magnificence by going back outside (**1** on the plan on page 15), and starting your tour with a look at the gatehouse. Basically thirteenth century, its four-sided projections on each side of the entrance give it a very ornamental appearance. The gatehouse has been greatly altered over the years, mainly in the nineteenth and early twentieth centuries when the custodian lived in it. This may explain why there are no front-facing windows except the slits at ground level, making the building look rather like a helmet with its visor down.

Originally there was a drawbridge, which could be hauled up so that its end rested just below the row of corbels (projecting stones) over the gate. In that position the drawbridge would have acted as an additional obstacle to attackers. The slits in the walls at the front of the gatehouse gave views out in all directions, allowing the gatekeeper to survey the approaches to the castle and look out along the south curtain wall on either side of him. Similarly the slits in the sides of the gate passage provided him with a further means of keeping an eye on people coming into the castle.

A castle's gatehouse was always seen as a vulnerable point, precisely because it had to contain a gate, and was therefore heavily defended. As you go through into the castle, you will see the grooves for the portcullis. The grooves come only part of the way down the walls, ending at the stone string course. The lower sections of the portcullis must have been a few inches narrower than the upper ones, which rested on the string course, and when lowered would have been held in position at ground level by a socket or bolt. There was once another gate at the far end of the entrance passage.

Once you have passed through the gatehouse, turn right and then right again into one of the guardrooms. They have no latrines or fireplaces, suggesting that the porter rarely stayed in one of them for long, only when a visitor, or an

unexpected emergency, brought him to the gate. The chambers above, accessible by stairs from either side of the entrance passage, have been altered out of all recognition from their earlier condition. But it is worth going up, if only to see the grooves in which the portcullis was lowered and raised.

Domestic Quarters
Fifteenth-century visitors, who satisfied the gatekeeper of their trustworthiness and were allowed to pass the gatehouse, would have found themselves in an open space surrounded by towers – a striking effect. In front of them was the looming bulk of the keep. To their right were the

SKYSCAN BALLOON PHOTOGRAPHY

The castle towering over the River Coquet and the village, with the gatehouse on the left, the Montague Tower in the foreground, the keep on the right and the foundations of the collegiate church in the centre. Compare this view with the plan, pages 14-15

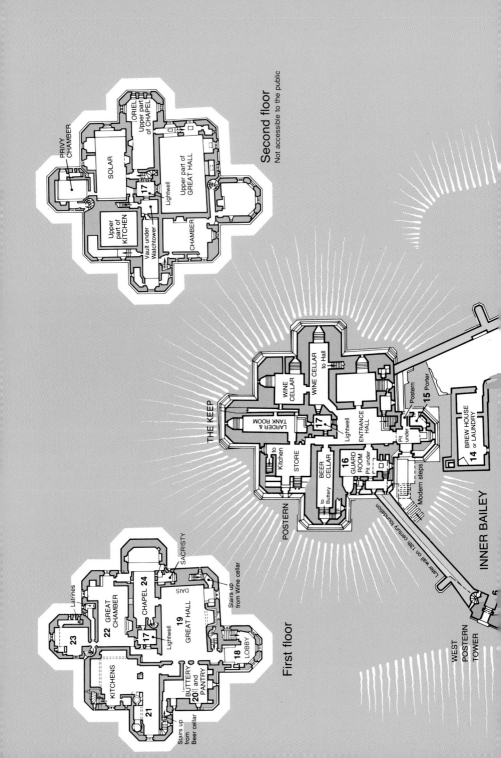

Second floor
Not accessible to the public

PRIVY
CHAMBER

ORIEL
Upper part
of CHAPEL

SOLAR

Upper
part of
KITCHEN

Vault under
Watchtower

17

Lightwell

Upper part of
GREAT HALL

CHAMBER

THE KEEP

WINE
CELLAR

WINE CELLAR
to Hall

LARDER &
TANK ROOM

17

Lightwell

STORE

to
Kitchen

BEER
CELLAR

ENTRANCE
HALL

Postern

15 Porter

16
GUARD
ROOM

Pit under

to
Buttery

Pit under

Modern steps

Later wall on 13th century foundation

POSTERN

INNER BAILEY

BREW HOUSE
14 or LAUNDRY

WEST
POSTERN
TOWER

First floor

Latrines

23

22 GREAT
CHAMBER

CHAPEL **24**

17

Lightwell

19
GREAT HALL

DAIS

SACRISTY

Stairs up
from Wine cellar

18

LOBBY

KITCHENS

21

20 BUTTERY
and PANTRY

Stairs up
from
Beer cellar

12th century
1191 – 1214
1249 – 1310
Early 14th century
Late 14th and early 15th century
Late 15th century
16th century
Modern
Uncertain, probably 14th century

Metres
0 10 20 30 40

Feet
0 50 100 150

TURRET

EAST
POSTERN

STABLES
11

WELL HOUSE
12

MONTAGUE
TOWER

13

Later wall on 13th century foundation

OUTER BAILEY

GATEHOUSE

GUARDROOM

GUARDROOM

BRIDGE

1

CHURCH

Passage

9

G below

LION
TOWER

7

LARDER

BUTTERY

PANTRY

HALL
4

AISLE

2nd Hearth

1st Hearth

Norman
fireplace

2

Cellar

SOLAR

ABOVE

CHAPEL

Pit
under

CARRICKFERGUS
TOWER

3

Later wall on 12th century foundation

The tower on the left was the gateway to the hall, solar, chapel and cellar. The Lion Tower on the right was the state entrance to the hall for visitors

Grey Mare's Tail Tower and the Montague Tower. And to their left was a row of buildings with two entrances, each of which had a tower above it. Those buildings, which formed a single block, stood at the heart of the castle, consisting as they did of the domestic quarters for the lord and his family.

To understand what today looks like a complicated tangle of ruins, it is best to start by making your way towards the tower gateway in the southwest corner (**2** on the plan on page 15). Look up into the tower gateway as you get closer to it. A graceful structure, with its pinnacle at the top, its upper floors were connected by a spiral staircase, part of which you will be able to see if you look up from the cellar; it terminates in a vault like an opened umbrella. Its first floor was a single room with a plainer but still handsome vault

over it – viewed from the bailey its outlines are still visible on the walls. This could have been a private chapel, but might equally well have been a superior guest chamber.

At ground level the tower has four doorways. The door on the left gave access to the west end of the chapel for soldiers and servants (there was a gallery above for their lords). The chapel is mostly of the early fourteenth century, and is identified as a chapel by the piscina (the basin where the priest washed his sacred vessels) set into the south wall. The hole in the ground towards the west end of the chapel probably marks the spot where the font stood. Warkworth was a domestic residence as well as a power base for the Claverings and Percys, so there must have been occasions when children were born and baptised here.

Nearly all castles had a chapel, fitted out as lavishly as their lords could afford. The Percys were rich, and the chapel fittings owned by the first earl and Hotspur included a silver-gilt alms dish, a silver-gilt crucifix, two great silver-gilt candlesticks, and a black velvet cope, the borders of which were set with pearls.

Straight ahead from the outer bailey, the tower's west door will bring you into an open space which was occupied by a cellar, with a door at its south end opening into a passage which once led to the ground floor of the Carrickfergus Tower **3**. You can see the bases of three columns that supported the room above: the great chamber or solar, the lord's private apartment.

Look up at the west wall of the solar (which occupied the whole of the first-floor space over the cellar) and note the fireplace with the remains of a chimney breast over it and two windows to the right of it. With the river below, this was the side of the castle least likely to be attacked, so here it was safest to make holes in or through the wall. Cross over to that wall and walk up the stairs built into its thickness. Looking ahead of you from the top of the stairs, you can see in the southwest corner a doorway giving access to a little chamber beyond. This was probably the closet in which royal money from Scotland was said to have been put for safe keeping at the time of Wallace's rebellion in 1297 – a position immediately next to the lord's chamber would certainly have been appropriate for what was in effect a large wall safe.

To the left of the closet, in the south wall of the solar, are two more doorways. Both lead into the Carrickfergus Tower, that on the right directly through a passage; that on the left via a staircase going up to the tower's second floor. One can see into the tower from outside the castle. It is very domestic in character, with a fireplace on each floor and plenty of windows. It was evidently intended to act as an extension of the solar for the lord and his family.

Further to the left, before the collapse of the floor, there would have been a way into a gallery above the west end of the chapel, reserved for the Claverings (who built most of this part of the castle) and later for the Percys when they attended mass. Looking back to the way you came in, you can see a door into the first floor of the tower under which you walked.

Now make your way back down the stairs and into the hall **4**. Lesser men would have come into the hall through another of the doorways under the tower, but you can go as the lord would have done, straight from his private rooms to the place where he showed his public face. Its earliest masonry dates from the mid twelfth century. At that date lords usually ate their meals with their followers. As time passed they tended to want greater privacy, and withdrew into rooms like the solar, where they could eat with their families and friends. But on important occasions, such as a religious festival or the start of a campaign, they still dined in hall, displaying their greatness with all the external signs of wealth and power.

In a castle such as Warkworth the hall would have been hung with tapestries. Sitting on a dais, the lord would have had a noble show of plate spread out behind and on either side of him. Hotspur, for instance, could have laid out such treasures as a great golden bowl with a cover, the knob of which was enamelled with ivy leaf and the Percy fetterlock, twenty-four silver goblets, twenty-four silver dishes, six dozen silver spoons and four silver-gilt basins.

From the fact that there is a Norman fireplace in its south wall, it seems likely that the hall was originally built on an east–west alignment, so that the lord sat

The site of the buttery, pantry and kitchen with the west postern gate beyond

with his back to the curtain wall, with the fire to his right. But later, probably early in the thirteenth century, the design of the hall was changed, so that it lay along the curtain wall instead of extending out into the bailey. The lord's place came to be at its south end and a fire now burned in an open hearth in front of him – the bases of two hearths can still be seen. His men sat at tables extending lengthwise down the hall.

The realigned hall had an aisle on its eastern side – you can see the bases of two of the aisle columns. But even so the hall was never very big – excessive size would have defeated one of its purposes: creating a feeling of togetherness, linking the lord and his men. Looking down to the other end of the hall, the lord could see the entrances to the buttery, pantry and kitchen. The central doorway led to the kitchen, probably via a passage divided

from the pantry by a timber screen. This would have permitted splendid moments of ceremony when servants processed through the three doors bearing the lord's meat, bread and drink, and the company stood up in honour of their master's food.

If you pass out of the north end of the hall, you will come to the buttery, on the left, where the drink was stored, and the pantry, where bread was kept, to the right of it. Next comes the larder, or meat store, against the west wall, and finally the kitchen **5**. In the latter you can see a hole below the west wall where slops and dirty water could be thrown out, with a stone cistern for storing water next to it. The remains of what may have been another cistern can be seen built into the foundations of the wall opposite. In the northwest corner are the remains of a bread oven with a fireplace next to it, both made of brick.

Walk through the passage alongside the kitchen until you come to the postern, with its tower above **6**. The word postern implies a bolt-hole in time of siege, or a means of making unexpected attacks on besiegers. This one could have served such purposes, though it was not designed for quick exits and entrances. It had a portcullis that was raised and lowered from the chamber over the gate (the lower part of the portcullis grooves were blocked at a later date). It is unusually wide and its position next to the kitchen suggests that it was also, or even primarily, a tradesmen's entrance, through which supplies could be brought in from the village and the lord's estates, without having to go round to the front and in through the gatehouse.

If you turn back now you can admire the Lion Tower **7**.

Lion Tower

This tower served as a state entrance to the hall for visitors. There was heraldry everywhere in medieval England, on tombs, weapons, seals, rings, plate, church vestments, the walls of monasteries, churches and houses, wherever space could be found for it – it was a way of proclaiming one's rank and importance. So it was with this tower – it became very prominent indeed when it was extended upwards in the fifteenth century, acquiring additional space for accommodation in the process. The Percy lion – very worn now – is carved on the central boss of the vault under its arch.

Externally you can see the great stone lion supported by brackets, and above it two shields, now sadly decayed (illustration page 16). The one on the left bore fusils, another Percy badge, that on

If it had been completed the collegiate church would have stood on the foundations that can be seen between the Lion Tower and the keep

the right the luces of the Lucys, whose coat of arms was also a visual pun on their family name. Caps of state over the shields completed the effect. All these sculptures would have been brightly coloured, leaving visitors in no doubt at all about the identity and standing of their host.

Collegiate Church

The Lion Tower was a way into the hall from the outer bailey. It was also a way out of the hall into what was intended to be one of the most splendid additions to the castle, and a notable sign of Percy greatness, the collegiate church **8**, the foundations of which can be seen stretching across the middle of the outer bailey. A number of late medieval castles had such churches, probably following the example of Edward III's foundation at Windsor, their purpose being to maintain a number of clergy (a "college") who would pray for the souls of their founders, and for the founders' ancestors and descendants. This one was almost certainly "our chantry lately founded in our castle at Warkworth," which the second earl referred to in 1429, being intended by him as a family mausoleum where prayers would be offered for his father and grandfather.

The church was never finished, but was laid out to have a nave and two aisles, two transepts, a tower above its crossing, and a quire at the east end. The ground slopes up from west to east, and presumably the east end was deliberately raised to make space for the crypts below. There are two of these, which would have been entered by stairs from the north transept. *Approach the crypts at ground level from the north; do not try to climb down the surviving masonry.* The larger crypt, which is supported by a column and has three windows (two facing north and one south) would have been intended to hold tombs, to which the earl and his family could descend in solemn procession to pray on the anniversaries of the deaths of their forebears. The smaller, which is lit by three windows, was probably intended for a priest, where he could robe and keep church plate and vestments.

The west to east slope also allowed space for a passage under the church **9**. There was much that was theatrical about medieval castles. It was doubtless intended that visitors to Warkworth should see it as a sequence of towers. Having entered under the lofty gatehouse, directly in front of them they would see the crossing tower of the collegiate church, and immediately behind that the spectacular mass of the keep. And then, in a further dramatic gesture, as they were taken towards the keep, with the church apparently blocking the way, they would suddenly find themselves being taken underneath it. However, you are advised to leave the keep till later, and look at the other buildings in the outer ward first.

East Curtain Wall and its buildings

Immediately to the east of the collegiate church is a jumble of ruins, the foundations of now unidentifiable buildings. But behind them stands the Grey Mare's Tail Tower **10** which is well worth inspection. On the west side of the castle, protected by the river and a steep slope, you saw the domestic buildings. But on the east side the castle was more open to attack, and the buildings here are of a more military character.

The Grey Mare's Tail Tower has been dated to early in the fourteenth century, that is, to a time when Scottish raids were common occurrences in Northumberland. Its interest is more than military, however, for in it you can see something of the castle's sanitary arrangements. To the left of the entrance at ground level is a double latrine slotted into the angle between the curtain wall and the tower's north side.

It is not known for certain why this tower was so named, but its position near the stables may have something to do with it. Looked at from the outside, each of the tower's five faces is divided by what appears to be a single long slit in the stonework. But on the inside you can see that each slit covers two deep embrasures, one above the other, through which longbows or crossbows could be fired. They are skilfully placed so as to command the face of the curtain wall as well as the approaches to the castle. In two embrasures, a timber crossbeam is still in place. By one of these beams, and behind an iron grill, you can see an unusual piece of amateur sculpture, the work of a devout soldier (or desperate prisoner) who carved crucifixes and human heads on the under side. His technical skill may have been limited, but he left fascinating evidence of his religious faith.

Going back south along the curtain wall, you come next to the site of the stables **11**. These were the medieval equivalent of garages – practically everything in the way of speed, mobility and transport which people use cars and lorries for now, in the Middle Ages were quite literally a matter of horsepower. In the sixteenth century the fifth earl of Northumberland was reckoned to have up to twenty-seven horses in his stables at any one time, so it is not surprising that the Warkworth stables took up a lot of space. A two-storey structure, it probably stood directly against the curtain wall, with a flat or sloping pent roof over its top floor, which served as a store and granary. No doubt it held oats and hay for horses as well as wheat for men and women.

In front of the stables is the wellhouse – a vital factor in the life of any castle. At least 60 feet (18.3m) deep and lined with stone, the well stood in a building which would have protected the water supply from dust and debris, as well as from missiles in time of siege. Water was probably raised in buckets by men turning a windlass. On the north side you can see the beginnings of three conduits which would have taken the water direct to buildings where it was needed or to cisterns for storage. Medieval people may have been lacking in precise scientific knowledge, but they were capable of great sophistication in matters of engineering and sanitation.

To the south of the stables is the east postern, and then, in the southeast corner, the Montague Tower. Built, or at least begun, in the 1460s by John Neville, Lord Montague, when he also had the title Earl of Northumberland, it served both for defence and accommodation. The window on the ground floor allows for a lookout along the east curtain wall, and over the nearby postern gate. But the three upper floors, each consisting of a single room with handsome two-light windows and a fireplace (the second-floor room has a latrine as well), would certainly have been intended to provide accommodation, doubtless for important guests.

Outside the tower, where it joins the south curtain wall, you can see remains of stairs that gave access to the tower itself and to the top of the curtain wall. The latter was rebuilt in the 1530s, and needed further attention in the eighteenth century, when most of it was taken down. The buildings the foundations of which you can see immediately behind the curtain wall cannot now be identified.

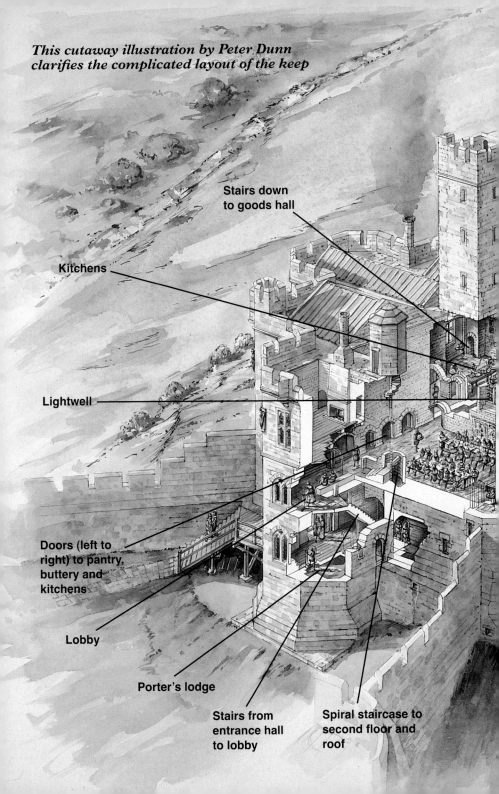

This cutaway illustration by Peter Dunn clarifies the complicated layout of the keep

Stairs down to goods hall

Kitchens

Lightwell

Doors (left to right) to pantry, buttery and kitchens

Lobby

Porter's lodge

Stairs from entrance hall to lobby

Spiral staircase to second floor and roof

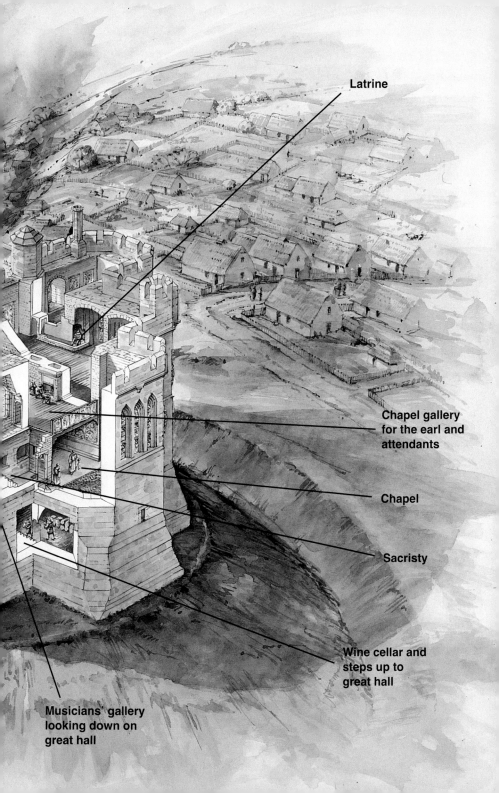

Latrine

Chapel gallery
for the earl and
attendants

Chapel

Sacristy

Wine cellar and
steps up to
great hall

Musicians' gallery
looking down on
great hall

A Visit to the Keep

The approach to the keep was by the passage under the uncompleted church

Warkworth was in effect two castles. The previous chapter took you around the first castle: basically a typical medieval castle, developing over several centuries and being continually adapted to meet the needs of changing times. But the second castle, the great keep, was built according to a single plan, and probably in a single extended building campaign, in the 1380s and 1390s.

Why was such a structure thought necessary? Double castles were not unknown. Warkworth would often have been left to its constable, himself usually an important local figure, with his own household and retinue. When the earl came, although he could occupy a room or suite of rooms in the existing castle (in the sixteenth century the sixth earl was said to have slept in the "lityll chamber over the gaytts," probably a room in the Lion Tower), he may have come to prefer to have separate quarters for himself and his men, leaving the constable where he was. And if he was visited by, for example, the Bishop of Durham or the Neville Earl of Westmorland, the Earl of Northumberland could now offer him one castle for his lodging, while himself occupying another on the same site. But above all the keep was surely a spectacular gesture by the first earl, of his confidence in himself, in his wealth and following in the North, and in the greatness and permanence of the Percy family.

Step back in time – December 1532

Visiting any old building always requires an effort of imagination. (See the plans on pages 14 and 15 and the illustration on the centre pages.) As you start your tour of the keep, you may like to imagine that you are an important guest at the festivities known to have been held at Warkworth at the end of 1532. Henry, the sixth earl, will spend Christmas here, and as he is on bad terms with his wife, her place as hostess will be taken by the earl's sister Margaret, who has been invited to stay with her husband, the Earl of Cumberland. As there are two castles, the Earl of Northumberland will occupy one, the keep, while the Earl of Cumberland's party stay in the other, in the outer bailey.

You are the Earl of Northumberland's guest, so having entered the castle through the gatehouse, and seen your horse taken away to the stables, you are led towards the keep. You were invited for supper which will be eaten at about 5pm, but your horse made good speed and you arrived early, so there is still a little light in the sky as men with torches conduct you through the passage **9** under the unfinished church. As you turn towards the steps up to the keep, you pass another building on your right **14**. It smells as if it might be a brewery, but in the fading light you cannot be sure.

As you walk up to the great mass of the keep you can just see that this splendid tower rests on a base of what looks like older masonry, the foundation of an earlier tower on the same site. But you don't stop to look for long. The porter, looking out of his lodge **15**, has seen you coming and is expecting you. The portcullis remains up, and you are allowed to enter. The wooden floor may feel a little springy under your feet as soon as you enter. You do not know, though you may guess, that there is a pit beneath and, had you broken in as an enemy, the removal of a bolt would have made that floor a trap into which you would have fallen. But nothing like that happens, and as you have arrived early, and have never seen this magnificent tower before, the porter suggests that you have a quick look around downstairs.

Turning away from the door, and from the postern facing it which gives access to the wall beyond, you come into a hallway. It is dark here, so the porter puts the lamp he is carrying in the niche cut into the wall on the left-hand side. Its flickering light helps you see your way about. Nearly all the rooms down here are store rooms, the porter tells you, though not the first room you come to on the left **16**. This, he explains (while also cursing whoever left the bowl of a stone font on the floor – perhaps one day the servants will remember to take it up to the chapel), is a guardroom where men-at-arms can assemble in times of danger. And below the floor there is a dungeon, really no more than a hole in the ground under the floorboards. To be shut up in that would be no joke.

But for men on duty there are basic comforts, and the porter invites you to walk up the steps to the door beyond the trapdoor. Looking inside you can see in the gloom that this little annex contains a latrine and fireplace. And as you step down again you notice that its door shuts from the outside, so that should the need arise the annex could be used as a small prison.

Walking out again into the hallway you notice a very bare-looking room on the other side of the entrance hall. Peering in you decide that this must be a store room as it has no fireplace. Piled up against the walls are what look like guns and pieces of

Cutaway illustration by Peter Dunn showing the lightwell and demonstrating how water collected from it was used to flush out the latrine shafts

Water from the lightwell could be collected in a tank or diverted to flush out the latrine shafts

armour, but in the fading light it is difficult to be sure.

The porter collects the lamp from its niche and leads you on down the passage, away from the entrance. Passing a doorway on your left – the way into the beer cellar, your guide observes over his shoulder – you turn right and find yourself looking at a structure which, the porter proudly explains, is a source of both light and water. It is a lightwell, open to the sky above and pierced by windows which admit air and a little daylight to parts of the keep which would otherwise be dark. And, extending from the top to the bottom of the keep, it also serves as a funnel for rainwater.

The water, you learn to your amazement, can be directed into a large tank at the foot of the lightwell, but normally it flows into a pipe and flushes out the discharge shafts from latrines on the floors above. Of course, the rainwater is hardly going to be clean enough for drinking or cooking but, once it has had time to settle, the contents of the tank can be used for washing floors or cleaning out other drains and latrines, like the one next to the guardroom which you saw earlier. You shake your head in wonder at such ingenuity – this must be why Warkworth smells less than other castles you have visited.

As you stand there in near darkness, with the light from the lamp shimmering on the water in the tank, the porter explains how the other rooms down here are laid out. There are two wine cellars to the east of the lightwell, where wine is stored in barrels and drawn off as required. On the opposite side is the general store and distribution point, piled high with sacks and boxes. And in between, facing the cistern at the north end of the keep, is the larder, the coldest room in the building and an appropriate place to store meat. Not that there is much in here now, of course – it is nearly all upstairs being cooked for this evening's meal.

No, indeed, the porter says in answer to your question, the goods stored down here did not come into the keep the way you came, but through a postern in the west wall of the store room. Nor will they go out the way you will shortly be going upstairs, for the first wine cellar, the beer cellar and the store room all have their own stairs, connecting them directly with the rooms above. Supplying a castle like Warkworth for Christmas is a tremendous business, and the earl's officers have been working flat out, getting food, drink, firewood, and other necessaries sent in from their master's estates. The wine came from Newcastle, the only place they could get it in these parts, but almost everything else – hay, grain, meat, beer, pots and pans for cooking, bedding – came from somewhere on the earl's lands in Northumberland, brought here in carts borrowed from his tenants. The trout and

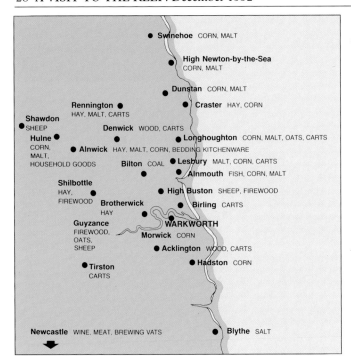

Sources of supplies for Warkworth in the early 1530s

Swinehoe CORN, MALT

High Newton-by-the-Sea CORN, MALT

Dunstan CORN, MALT

Rennington HAY, MALT, CARTS

Craster HAY, CORN

Shawdon SHEEP

Hulne CORN, MALT, HOUSEHOLD GOODS

Denwick WOOD, CARTS

Longhoughton CORN, MALT, OATS, CARTS

Alnwick HAY, MALT, CORN, BEDDING KITCHENWARE

Bilton COAL

Lesbury MALT, CORN, CARTS

Alnmouth FISH, CORN, MALT

Shilbottle HAY, FIREWOOD

High Buston SHEEP, FIREWOOD

Brotherwick HAY

Birling CARTS

Guyzance FIREWOOD, OATS, SHEEP

WARKWORTH

Morwick CORN

Acklington WOOD, CARTS

Tirston CARTS

Hadston CORN

Newcastle WINE, MEAT, BREWING VATS

Blythe SALT

salmon which the earl gives to lucky guests could hardly be fresher, for they were caught in the River Coquet, next to the castle.

It is dark by the time the porter has told you all this and you make your way back to the entrance. There is a small chamber a couple of steps up from the foot of the stairs. The porter tells the scurvy varlet who sits in it to take you upstairs, and then returns to his post.

Passing a doorway at the top of the stairs, you come to a lobby **18** with window seats, and stone benches before another door. There is a fire burning here, and as you are too wise in the ways of the world to expect to be admitted to the earl's presence at once – really important people show their greatness by keeping lesser folk waiting, or even refusing to see them at all – you sit down to wait while an attendant goes to announce you.

Looking out through the not very clear glass in the handsome windows, the light of torches in the outer bailey shows other guests arriving. One of these is old Sir Marmaduke, and as soon as he reaches the lobby you know that he is going to tell you all over again how he won the battle of Flodden single-handed. So you decide to risk being found where you should not be, and see how the preparations for the banquet are getting on.

Slipping into the great hall **19**, you find a few servants laying tables, and one or two other early guests sitting on benches, listening to the musicians practising in the gallery at the east end. At the west end, to your left, there are three doors. The first two, you realise as you go through one of them, both open into what is really one large room **20**, containing the pantry, for bread, and the buttery, where the beer is made ready after being brought up the

The first-floor lobby with stone seats and a fireplace

Cooks at work in the great kitchen. Illustration by Ivan Lapper

stairs from the beer cellar below. Back you go into the great hall, and then in through the last of the three doors. This brings you into the kitchen – kitchens really, one large and one small.

To your left is a fireplace **21** with a bread oven on the left and a place for a cauldron on the right. But when you go into the great kitchen, with its ceiling high above you, the heat from the two huge fireplaces and the hubbub, as far too many cooks set about spoiling the broth, are overwhelming. You think you will peer into the cupboard on the left opposite the stairs down to the store, as this is probably where the spices which will enliven this evening's meal are kept. However, you beat a hasty retreat back to the entrance lobby when someone sloshes a bucket of water across the floor to wash all the scraps of food lying around there down the drain in the west wall, just missing your new shoes.

No sooner have you sat down again than the attendant reappears, to take you into the earl's presence. A short walk across the great hall, past the kitchen door, and through a short passage with the lightwell on your right, brings you to the great chamber **22**.

You see at once that this is a room designed for privacy and comfort. There are handsome windows in its north and east wall, the latter with a stone bench next to it, where two of the Countess of Cumberland's ladies-in-waiting sit bent over their needlework. It feels different under foot in here, with woven rush mats, and even one or two small carpets on the floor, instead of the loose rushes on which you walked as you crossed the great hall. And it smells different, too, as the great chamber is lit by candles made of beeswax, not of the tallow – rendered-down animal fat – used almost everywhere else in the castle. There is the Earl of Northumberland (looking ill as usual,

poor fellow), with his sister and brother-in-law, huddled in front of the fire.

The fireplace seems rather small for so fine a room, and you remember the porter telling you that next year the earl intends to have it replaced by a much larger one. Then you kiss the earl's hand, and as you stand talking you look round the room, admiring the furnishings – the tapestries on the walls, interspersed with portraits and pictures of saints, the cushions decorated with flowers and pomegranates, the silver plate on the sideboard. But all too soon an attendant comes to lead you to your bedroom, and with a low bow you withdraw.

You follow the servant in the direction away from the fireplace, through a narrow lobby with a doorway, obviously to stairs going up to a higher floor, on your left, and a passage to the right – a strong whiff tells you that there is a latrine at the end of this, but that does not bother you, because it is common knowledge that there is nothing like the smell of urine for keeping clothes-moths away.

You walk into what will be your bedroom tonight **23**. You must be very important in the earl's eyes, because you have it to yourself. Most people will have to share a room, and very often a bed – the four cooks, the porter told you, will have two beds between them, and all over the castle men will be sleeping wherever space can be found for them. But here there is privacy and comfort, with the draughts from the window offset by the blaze in the fireplace on the west side of the room. Opposite the fire is a passage which leads you to your own garderobe (latrine). You tidy your clothes, and then the servant comes back to summon you to the meal. You go back the way you came, and are shown to your place in the great hall.

There are two long trestle tables, covered with linen cloths, laid out side by side down the body of the great hall, with benches on each side of them. At the far end of the hall is a dais with another table on it. That is where the earl and his guests will sit. Your place is at the table on the left, just below the dais, with the wall behind you. But you do not sit down at once. The musicians in the gallery, led by the earl's trumpeter, play a fanfare; the three doors at the far end of the hall fly open and a procession of servants marches down the hall, carrying dishes of steaming food, which they set before the place where the earl will sit. And then another fanfare sounds and the Earl of Northumberland and his guests enter through the small doorway almost behind you, and take their places at the high table, the earl in the middle, his sister and the Earl of Cumberland (a dry old stick, you think) on either side of him. The earl's chaplain says grace, and after much ceremony, including a formal tasting to make sure that it is not poisoned, the meat is carved and distributed.

You are sitting down by now, and while all this is going on you can look about you. It is warm in here. Until quite recently, you gather, heat was provided by an open fire in a central hearth. But the earl wanted something better, and converted the second of the two windows in the wall opposite you into a fireplace with a chimney. The servants are kept busy feeding the fire with logs – wood, not coal, is burnt in here this evening, because the dust and smoke from coal might damage the hangings on the walls. These are indeed rather striking – one is embroidered to tell the story of Alexander the Great, another shows the birth of Venus.

In the light from countless tallow candles you can see the handsome two-light window opposite you. It is unusually long, but then this is a very high room, extending up to the roof of the keep. And you admire the way the hall is connected to the cellars below. From where you are sitting you can see the head of the stairs, and servants coming up with bottles of wine, which they leave on the stone ledge to the right of the window until needed.

In due course a waiter brings your food in a dish which he sets before you and your neighbour. Only very important people get a portion each but your rank is such that you have to share with only one other guest (further down the table there are men sharing in fours). Nothing very fancy, but plenty to drink and good beef, mutton, chicken, even duck, ladled out on to the chunks of dry bread, known as trenchers, which have been set before you. You talk to your neighbours, while the musicians play in the gallery, and you learn that there is trouble on the border and a campaign against the Scots may be imminent. So those *were* guns you saw piled up in the store room downstairs. And sure enough, there is the earl on his feet, making a speech of welcome, which turns into an appeal to the company for their support when the summons comes. Your family has served the Percys for generations, and warmed by the earl's food and drink, you know you will be there.

And then, as you finish eating, the trenchers are cleared away (soaked in gravy, they and any leavings will be given to the poor tomorrow), the salt cellars, goblets, knives and other things on the tables are removed, and finally the tablecloths are taken off and the tables are dismantled. While this is happening, you and the other guests have moved down to the west end of the hall, and are standing in orderly rows. The musicians sound another fanfare, the Earl and Countess of Cumberland leave for their quarters in the outer bailey, and then the Earl of Northumberland makes his departure, going out the way he came in, back into the great chamber.

On another occasion there might be dancing, or some other form of revelry, but this banquet, arranged in anticipation of a campaign, has been an all-male affair, apart from the Countess of Cumberland. And so the guests, too, depart, either for their homes or for their bedrooms. You follow an attendant back to your room, passing through an already deserted great chamber – clearly the earl has gone upstairs to bed.

A servant wakes you at an early hour so that you can attend a service in the chapel. With a torch in his hand he leads you back through the great chamber into the great hall, where through bleary eyes you notice that a few servants are still sleeping on the rush-covered floor, while others are putting up tables for breakfast. But you are not going to eat just yet. You follow your attendant down to the far end of the hall where, turning left, you find yourself in the chapel. At six o'clock in the morning it is still dark outside; no light comes in from the three-light window in front of you, or from the lightwell behind. But this is made up for by candles on the altar and in brackets on the walls.

The altar stands on a dais, the floor of which is covered with glazed tiles, something you do not recall seeing in these parts before. The candlelight reflects softly from the tiles, more brightly from the plate on the altar, and especially from the great silver cross in the middle.

Sounds from above indicate that there is a gallery over your head, and that the earl and his attendants have taken their places in it, looking down to the altar. The Earl of Cumberland and his household will worship in the older chapel next to the outer gatehouse.

As you wait for the service to begin you admire the painted stone statues in the niches which flank the window and the hangings on the walls – one shows the twelve prophets, another the twelve apostles. You can hear rustlings away to your right. There must be a sacristy round the corner where the earl's chaplain is robing himself and preparing his books and sacred vessels. Then he comes in, followed by an attendant or server, and you think of other things.

When the service is over, you eat some cold meat and drink a mug of ale in the great hall, and then a servant escorts you down to ground level. Your horse is waiting for you in the stable, and without further ado you mount, tip the groom holding the reins with a bent groat, and ride away. Warkworth Castle, you reflect as you leave, is indeed a noble castle.

The Hermitage

Exterior of the hermitage. The steps lead to the chapel which was cut into the cliff

Warkworth Hermitage is expected to be open from 10am to 6pm between 1 April and 30 September (*check at the castle ticket office*). To reach it, go out under the gatehouse, turn right and walk along the front of the castle until you come to a footpath. Follow this north (it is worth having a look at the interior of Carrickfergus Tower **3** as you pass – illustration page 44) until opposite the west postern **6**, when you will see another footpath on your left leading down to the River Coquet. You have ahead of you a very attractive walk of about half a mile, with the river on your right; on the other side of it are fields that were once enclosed

in the Warkworth deerpark – in 1512 it was said to contain 150 fallow deer.

Hunting was the favourite pastime of medieval lords and gentry, quite apart from being a useful source of meat, and there were few better ways for an Earl of Northumberland to make friends and influence people than to give them a day's sport. But although everything at Warkworth was to a greater or lesser extent bound up with the power of its lords, the hermitage was concerned with a sort of power different from that exercised in the castle or the hunting field.

As well as being a military stronghold and a centre for a great lordship,

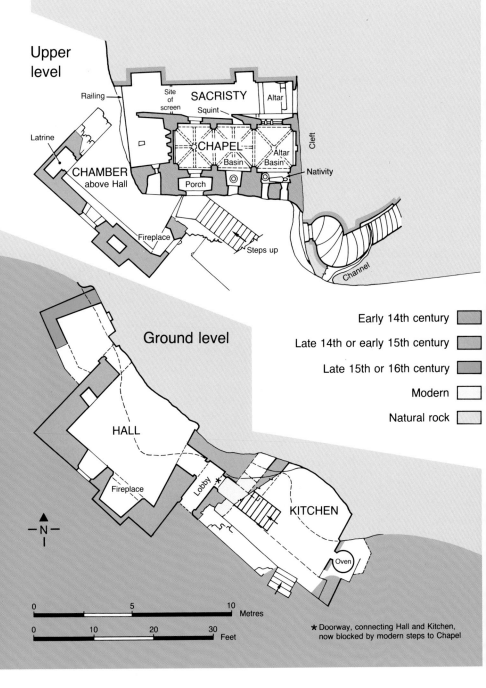

Upper level

Railing
Site of screen
SACRISTY
Altar
Squint
Latrine
CHAPEL
Altar
CHAMBER above Hall
Basin
Basin
Cleft
Nativity
Porch
Fireplace
Steps up
Channel

Ground level

HALL
Fireplace
Lobby
KITCHEN
Oven

N

Early 14th century
Late 14th or early 15th century
Late 15th or 16th century
Modern
Natural rock

0   5   10   Metres
0   10   20   30   Feet

★ Doorway, connecting Hall and Kitchen, now blocked by modern steps to Chapel

The hermitage chapel. On the left of the altar is the squint from the sacristy. Note also the basin on the right

Warkworth also had significant spiritual functions. The old castle and the first earl's keep both had chapels, and there were also the plans for a collegiate church in the outer ward. The purpose of all these structures was the same: the offering of prayers to God for the wellbeing of the lords of the castle, their forebears and successors, their families and followers, and ultimately for all Christian folk. Warkworth Hermitage, on the north bank of the Coquet, was another source of prayer and devotion.

Although he was free to move around, a hermit was essentially a religious solitary, giving himself to a life of prayer, for his own salvation and that of others. It is not known who the first hermit of

Warkworth was, or when he started to live at the hermitage, but it is likely that from the first he and his successors were supported by the lords of Warkworth. The hermitage was adapted over the centuries, however, and the hermit's responsibilities seem to have changed also, taking on a more secular quality. In the late fifteenth century he had a yearly stipend of 66 shillings and 8 pence (£3.33). But in the 1530s one George Lancastre was the hermit, and he was not only receiving a far higher salary, £13-6s-8d (£13.33), but was also acting as the sixth earl's agent on his Warkworth estate. In addition to his stipend, Lancastre had pasture for twelve cattle, a bull and two horses, and received twenty loads of firewood a year and a

Warkworth Castle as seen from the footpath along the River Coquet on the way back from the hermitage

catch of fish every Sunday, so he was living a life barely distinguishable from that of any other peasant farmer. It is hardly surprising that as a religious establishment the hermitage failed to survive the Reformation.

If it is possible to visit the hermitage a boat will ferry you over the river. A short walk along the river bank will bring you to stone steps to the hermitage: chambers, cut into the rock, in which the hermit performed his devotions, not necessarily

by himself. As they now survive the chambers are essentially an expression of the piety of the fourteenth century.

Entering at the upper level through a tiny porch, with a seat on each side, you pass under a door above which you can just see the remains of a carving of the crucifixion, with the Virgin and St John on either side of the cross.

The first chamber you enter is the *chapel* (see the plan on page 34). Although it all looks rather rough-hewn, you should admire the skill with which the stone has been cut, especially the columns against the walls and the ribs under the ceiling – had the sculptor made a mistake, he would not have been able to start again.

The altar stands at its usual position at the east end, with a niche behind it, either for relics or a statue. In the south wall, light comes in through a quatrefoil window in the bay next to the door, over a basin probably provided for the priest to clean his hands. The easternmost bay, which is lit by two small windows, contains not only a piscina, where the sacred vessels were washed, but also a fine, if worn, carving of the Nativity. The Virgin, holding the infant Jesus, lies outstretched, her head towards the altar, with an attendant behind her, while at her feet an ox looks on and Joseph sits in a weary posture.

With its rib vaults and sculpture of the Nativity, and the tracery window in its north wall which gives light to the sacristy, the chapel has an air of quality. It would have been relatively accessible to the outside world, and the lord of Warkworth, or members of his household, could have come here to pray with the hermit, or to make a confession to him, or to hear him preach.

On the far side of the chapel, above the doorway leading to the sacristy, is a shield

Worn carving of the Nativity in the bay to the right of the altar

carved with the instruments of the Passion – the cross itself, the nails, the spear, a lance with a sponge on it, hyssop leaves, and the crown of thorns. There were once words visible beneath it, a quotation from Psalm 69 – THEY GAVE ME GALL TO EAT: AND WHEN I WAS THIRSTY THEY GAVE ME VINEGAR TO DRINK – appropriate both to the Passion itself, and to the life of austere self-sacrifice which the hermit was expected to lead.

The *sacristy* was a place where the hermit could store his sacred vessels – there are two cupboards cut into the north wall. With its own altar at its east end, it was also a second, more secluded, place of prayer. Though he could look into the chapel, through the window or squint, perhaps to contemplate the altar or the carving of the Nativity, the hermit could practise his devotions alone in the sacristy.

There was a room at the west end of the chapel and sacristy, most of which has now collapsed, although its remains are accessible from the sacristy. It may have been intended to give access to the hermit as a man of prayer, in that the slits in the chapel's west wall would have allowed outsiders to look in when he celebrated mass, above all at the climactic moment of the elevation of the host – something the people of the later Middle Ages never tired of watching.

Looking out the other way, you can see something of the hermit's way of life in the structures below – they are also worth examining at ground level.

Some of the hermit's rooms are now lost. These were rather later than the rock-cut chambers, dating from the fifteenth and early sixteenth centuries. You can see that he had an upper room, backing on to the chapel and sacristy, and at ground level a hall and kitchen. The upper room had a latrine in its southwest corner, and a fireplace in the wall facing it. The hall had a large fireplace and a small cupboard. The kitchen was separated from the hall by an entrance lobby. The doorway through to the kitchen is now blocked by the modern steps up to the chapel. The circular base of the oven can be seen at the east end of the kitchen.

As he had pasture for livestock the hermit probably ate meat. His garden and orchard, which lay to the east of the hermitage, supplied him with fruit and vegetables. Both his hall and the room above it had windows looking out on to the river, and although these rooms could hardly be called luxurious, they clearly provided their occupant with at least modest comfort, as well as a beautiful setting for his secluded existence.

In an age often regarded as brutal and barbarous, the Earl of Northumberland lived in a style which was refined and, when necessary, splendid. Just down the river the earl's dependant, the hermit of Warkworth, also lived in circumstances better than first appearances might lead one to expect.

The Village

The village dominated by the castle, as seen from the tower of the church

A visit (without a car) to the village is well worth while. The main street, with fine Georgian houses on either side, runs down from behind the castle and widens in front of the parish church to make space for the marketplace.

As you approach from the south the church looks like a typical product of the later Middle Ages, with its fourteenth-century spire and broad windows. This is because what you see first is a south aisle which was added in the fifteenth century. But if you go in and through the aisle you will be in the finest and most complete Norman church in Northumberland – a structure at least as old as the oldest parts of the castle. Its architectural detail was greatly influenced by Durham Cathedral.

If you walk on down the road, as it swings round the east end of the church, you will come to the late fourteenth-century bridge – one of England's very few fortified bridges. The gatehouse at its southern end has a guard chamber on its west side, and the door opposite it probably gave access to the top of the wall which ran east and west of it.

These was no escaping the consequences of geography at Warkworth – its position in a border county made it liable to attack whenever England and Scotland were at war. So it was that this village acted as a sort of outer line of defence for the castle against attacks from the north.

This was not the only way in which the village and castle were linked. By the mid thirteenth century Warkworth was a

The parish church, most of which is as old as the earliest parts of the castle

borough, a privileged community, worth nearly £45 a year to its lords, who exploited it in every way they could. They took tolls from goods sold in the market, compelled the villagers to use the lord's oven and mill and pay him for doing so, and regulated their behaviour through a court, taking financial penalties from offenders. They also promoted a new settlement for fishermen and seamen on the north side of the Coquet, though it never really prospered.

Many of those who worked in the castle or on the home farm, which covered some 325 acres (132ha) in 1249, are likely to have come from the village, where every holding also had to provide one man to do two days' reaping each autumn or pay one penny instead.

Later on the home farm was largely

Late fourteenth-century fortified bridge which protected the village at its vulnerable river crossing

converted into a park, and the lords bought most of the products they needed, often from their own tenants, at Warkworth and further afield. The latter were still likely to have contributed many of the servants who cleaned rooms and stables, carried food, water and firewood, and did all the other chores that helped to make the castle habitable whenever the reigning Percy came into residence.

The relationship between castle and village was indeed that of master and servant. The great Percy lion on the north face of the keep, visible to anyone who looks south up the village street, still gives gives visual expression to the castle's domination of the community.

The great Percy lion on the north face of the keep

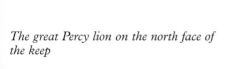

The Later History of Warkworth Castle

The Gray Mare's Tail Tower and the keep seen from outside the east curtain wall

"This worm-eaten hold of ragged stone"
(Henry IV, part II)

For the castle, and for its Percy lords, as well as for the hermitage, the Reformation marked a turning point. In 1557 the earldom of Northumberland was restored to the sixth earl's nephew, Thomas, by Queen Mary (1553–58). But like that queen, the new earl was a staunch Catholic, and in 1569 he took the disastrous decision to join the Rising of the Northern Earls against Elizabeth I (1558–1603). For the earl this led to his execution in 1572; for the castle to its systematic pillaging by the Queen's

servants, led by the capable but greedy and unscrupulous Sir John Forster. It looks as if in 1569 the earl had been planning substantial repairs, with many buildings being dismantled prior to their reconstruction. This made it all the easier to carry off timber and fittings – although the keep was spared, so clean a sweep did Forster make of the outer bailey that nearly forty years later it was thought noteworthy that he had actually left a small quantity of "decay'd tymber" in the old hall.

Like earlier monarchs, Elizabeth was prepared to restore the earldom to the Percys. But their religion continued to cause trouble for them. The eighth earl died in the Tower of London in 1585, where his successor was also confined for many years, suspected of involvement in the Gunpowder Plot. The castle was leased to a tenant, who neglected it – successive reports to the imprisoned earl told of roofs collapsed, timbers rotted, fittings stolen. Only the keep remained fairly intact, and this in spite of the fact that when James I and his court inspected Warkworth in 1617, they found goats and sheep in almost every room. King James himself gazed at the Percy lion carved on the north side of the keep and remarked, rather inconsequentially, "This lyone houldes upe this castle."

Perhaps it was sheer force of habit that held the castle up. With England and Scotland now under a single ruler, and the borders relatively peaceful, the Earls of Northumberland hardly needed two castles, even when they were in Northumberland to occupy them, so they concentrated their resources on Alnwick. The best use they could find for the Warkworth keep in the years round 1620 was as a place for manor courts, and as a store for oats grown on the nearby estates. The other buildings were left to moulder. Enough of the curtain walls remained for the Scots to occupy the castle during the Civil Wars of the 1640s.

The fact that the tenth earl took Parliament's side may have stopped them doing too much damage (one of them carved his name, G Ogle, and the date, 1644, on the inside of the kitchen's main oven in the keep), but Parliament's own forces were less restrained when they garrisoned the castle in 1648, and they did all the harm they could when they departed. By then Warkworth was just a picturesque ruin, and even the keep served no useful purpose. In 1672 the eleventh earl's widow gave its materials to John Clarke, one of the estate auditors.

Two hundred and seventy-two wagon loads of lead and timber were removed, to be reused in the house that Clarke was building at Chirton. The keep was left a shell.

And so it has largely remained, in spite of occasional proposals to restore it. In 1698, for instance, there were unfulfilled plans to bring the keep back into use, with a kitchen, larder, cellar and "a dineing room for sarvants" in the ground-level basements, and "a very noble dining rome" and "lodging romes" on the floors above. The line of Percy earls had ended in 1670, and the estates passed by marriage to the Dukes of Somerset, only to pass by another marriage to Sir Hugh Smithson, who took the name of Percy and founded another dynasty, this time as Dukes of Northumberland. Successive dukes were conscientious in their concern for their inheritance, at Warkworth as elsewhere. In the 1750s the sixteenth-century wall between the Montague Tower and the gatehouse was pulled down and rebuilt, while in 1832 the third duke was praised for having "invariably shown a disposition to preserve this grand specimen of the ancient baronial mansions of England from reckless dilapidation and decay."

But it was the fourth duke who did most for the castle. In the 1850s he financed excavations which brought the remains of the collegiate church to light again, and he also employed the architect Anthony Salvin to work on the keep, apparently intending to refurbish the hall so that manor courts could be held in it. The cost of reroofing the entire structure caused the plan to be dropped, but not before Salvin had put new roofs on the south projection and the chambers over the buttery and pantry, and had refaced the entrance to the keep and much of the stonework round it. The top-floor rooms (*not accessible to the public*) which Salvin

Looking over the dry moat to the Carrickfergus Tower and the gatehouse

had reroofed were sometimes used for picnics by the duke and his friends when they made excursions from Alnwick.

Alterations were also made to the gatehouse to provide a residence for a porter or custodian, one of whose jobs was to show visitors around. One custodian supplemented his income by selling game, so that sightseers were liable to find the gatehouse festooned with dead pheasants and rabbits.

Further excavations were carried out in the 1890s, this time uncovering some of the foundations along the east curtain. But the costs of maintenance were great, and when the Office of Works was empowered to take ancient monuments into guardianship, the Duke of Northumberland was one of the landowners who placed what had been their family seats in the keeping of the nation. Warkworth came into the custody of the Office of Works in 1922, eventually passing to English Heritage.